P

MW01124162

THE ORIGIN OF
FUTURISM
and
PRETERISM

Paul Owen

~~~~~~~~~~~~~~~~~~~~~~~~~~

PART TWO

THE TRAGIC AFTERMATH
OF FUTURISM

Charles A. Jennings

The Origin of Futurism and Preterism
and
The Tragic Aftermath of Futurism

Truth in History Ministries –
the evangelistic outreach of
The Bible Educator Ministry
P.O. Box 808
Owasso, Oklahoma 74055-0808
web site: www.truthinhistory.org
E-mail: charles@truthinhistory.org

ISBN – 978-0-9777039-3-7

Printed in the United States of America
September 2006

TABLE OF CONTENTS

THE ORIGIN OF FUTURISM AND PRETERISM

SECTION ONE - The Futurist and Preterist Views 1

SECTION TWO - The Development of Preterism and Its Interpretation of the Second Coming of Christ 20

Christ's Second Coming and Unfulfilled Prophecies 25

SECTION THREE - Unfulfilled Prophecy as of 70 AD 30

Misunderstanding and Misapplication of Scripture 37

By Paul Owen

* * * * * * * * * * * * * * * * * *

THE TRAGIC AFTERMATH OF FUTURISM

The Definition of Futurism 44

The Development of Futurism 45

False Hope 50

False Predictions 57

The Antichrist 58

Seventy Weeks of Daniel 61

The Two Witnesses 63

The Tragic Aftermath of Futurism 65

By Charles A. Jennings

FOREWORD

A few years ago, I wrote a small booklet titled *An Unchangeable Framework & A Firm Foundation* that included a chapter dealing with Preterism and Futurism. This booklet amplifies somewhat those brief comments relating to Preterism and presents an overview of it for your study.

I consider this topic of great importance and trust this small work will arouse your interest enough to investigate carefully all sides of this issue.

The information contained herein is a brief introduction to the origin of the Futurist and Preterist views of prophecy. It concerns itself with the interpretation and fulfillment of prophecy and not with the teaching of the "fundamentals of the faith." The term "fundamentals of the faith" can be condensed to the confession – "Jesus Christ is Lord!" Hopefully, all who read these pages, whatever their persuasion of prophecy, would say "Amen" to that.

It should be noted that this author does not hold to Preterism or Futurism, but yields himself to the Historicist viewpoint.

Paul Owen

PART ONE

THE ORIGIN OF FUTURISM AND PRETERISM

by Paul Owen

SECTION ONE

This booklet falls naturally into three sections. The first section is the most important because it addresses the origin of both the Futurist and Preterist views of prophecy.

Section Two will show the progression of the development of Preterism, from the period of the early church down through the Reformation. While there are divisions among Preterists as to certain of their dogmas, most hold to the belief that Christ's Second Coming has already occurred, that all of prophecy has been fulfilled, and that we are now in the Kingdom. This section will provide numerous Bible passages that offer sufficient Biblical support for the view that the Second Coming of Christ as foretold in Scripture has not yet occurred.

The Third Section will submit an Old Testament prophecy that puts to rest the Preterist's theory of the early fulfillment of all prophecy. It will conclude with two examples of the Preterists' misunderstanding or misapplication of Scripture.

The history of Futurism and Preterism should cause any thinking Christian flirting with either to take a serious in-depth look at both schools of prophecy and Scripture.

Prophetic Schools Defined

For those who find the terms Historicism, Preterism, and Futurism ambiguous, the definitions are herein supplied:

Historicism teaches that Jesus Christ's "unveiling" to the Apostle John, that comprises the Book of Revelation, renders an on-going history of the "church," or "called-out-ones," from the time of John until the Second Advent.

Preterism generally attempts to place the fulfillment of all prophecy at the fall of Jerusalem in 70 AD, yet some Preterists look at fulfillment when Pagan Rome fell in 410 AD.

Most Preterists are of the Post-Millennial school and believe the "called-out-ones" will eventually, through preaching of the Gospel and power of the Holy Spirit, convert the whole world to Christianity. Because that process could take 100, 1000, or 5000 years, no miscalculations are possible.

Futurism places events prophesied in Chapters 4 through 19 of the Book of Revelation into the future at the end of the Christian era. The term "Futurism" is often found as a part of the longer title "Dispensational, Pre-Trib Rapture, Futurist." One may use any of the individual designations to refer to the whole, which is often done. By their own words, it is evident that most Futurists are Pre-Trib Rapturists, and most Rapturists are Futurists. Both share their belief in Dispensationalism.

This booklet focuses on the prophetic question of Futurism, not on the Pre-Trib Rapture issue because many others have adequately covered that study. Mr. Dave MacPherson has done excellent work in researching that question, and his books are readily available.

Where We Are Today

For the past 50 or 60 years, Christian bookstores have carried the usual Bibles and books on Christian living. However, for the most part, their Bible study themes and their books concerning prophecy were of the Dispensational, Pre-Trib Rapture, Futurist point of view. This was the popular view during that time, because as history will substantiate, the high-water mark of the Futurist teaching was reached during the first half of the twentieth century. During that era, many events came to pass that seemed to add credence to their theory.

In 1897, as a starting point, Mr. Theodore Herzl organized the World Zionist Movement; the Scofield Reference Bible was published in 1907; November, 1917, the Balfour Declaration pledged the British government to the establishment of a Jewish national home in Palestine; December 11, 1917, British forces took Palestine, including Jerusalem, from the Turks; from the 1930's and the rise of Benito Mussolini, many potential anti-Christs have risen; in 1948, the UN partitioned Palestine, forming the Israeli state; and the six-day war of 1967 gave Israeli forces the capital city of Jerusalem. However, these events did not bring about the anticipated rapture.

What has generated this recent interest in Preterism? It appears that there have been an increasing number of ministers, scholars, and writers who are producing books espousing the Preterist viewpoint and pointing out the obvious errors and flaws of Futurism. Perhaps there is also a growing number of Pre-Trib Rapturists who have become weary of not seeing some of their treasured prophecies come to pass, causing the Futurists to look elsewhere for answers. For example, the Pre-Trib Rapturists taught that when the UN gave Palestine to the Jews in 1948, the rapture would occur and that the last seven years of the Prophet Daniel's tribulation time-clock would tick off. But seven years passed, and another seven years passed, and no rapture. Then they began to teach that for the Jews to really be in possession of the land, they must hold the Capital City, Jerusalem. This came about as a result of the 1967 War. Surely then the rapture would happen, and the last seven years of tribulation would tick off. History is a witness to what did *not* happen.

As a result of these miscalculations, it appears that some teachers, preachers, and other knowledgeable individuals of the Pre-Trib Futurist school have concluded that there was undoubtedly something amiss with their eschatology, and they are looking into another viewpoint.

Both the Futurists and the Preterists spare no words in attacking the other's position. They have been at odds for years, but the verbal fisticuffs seem to have intensified during the past decade. Their thinking seems to be that if they can prove the other wrong, then that automatically proves their position to be correct. Not true. The Historicist believes they are both in error.

Historicism: The Faith of Our Fathers

In the following pages, numerous quotations from distinguished authors and church scholars will be found. Because of their schooling and/or unique positions in history, they have earned the right to speak with authority on this subject. Historicism is a viewpoint that dates back to the earliest centuries of the Church but seems to be almost forgotten today among the opposing schools of prophetic interpretation. There is a plethora of material espousing Futurism, an abundance of books promoting Preterism, but scant mention of Historicism today.

In 1887, Dr. H. Grattan Guinness, DD., F.R.A.S., English scholar, preacher, writer and lecturer, wrote *Romanism and the Reformation – From the Standpoint of Prophecy.*

In this book, which was reprinted in 1967, he devoted three chapters to the overview of those who interpret prophecy: Pre-Reformation Interpreters, Interpreters of the Reformation and Post-Reformation Interpreters. He quotes from scores of writers, preachers and historians who were of the Historicist school of thought. Excerpts from his works bear repeating within these pages. Following are quotations from Lecture V, pages 112-114 of the above-mentioned book:

> With many varieties as to detail we find there have existed, and still exist, *two great opposite schools of interpretation*, the Papal and the Protestant, or the *futurist* and the *historical*. The latter regards the prophecies of Daniel, Paul and John as fully and faithfully setting forth *the entire course of Christian history;* the former as dealing chiefly with *a future fragment of time as its close.*[1]

> It is held by many that the *historic* school of interpretation is represented only by a *small modern section of the Church*. We shall show that *it has existed from the beginning*, and includes the *larger part* of the greatest and best teachers of the Church for 1800 years. We shall show that the *Fathers* of the Church belonged to it; that the most learned medieval commentators belonged to it, that the *confessors, reformers and martyrs* belonged to it, that it has included a vast multitude of erudite expositors of later times. We shall show that all these have held to the *central truth* that prophecy *faithfully mirrors the Church's history as a whole, and not merely a commencing or closing fragment of that history. . .*[2]

---

1. H. Grattan Guinness, DD., F.R.A.S., <u>Romanism and the Reformation – From the Standpoint of Prophecy,</u> Blackwood, New Jersey; Old Fashioned Prophecy Magazine, 1967, pp. 112-113
2. H. Grattan Guinness, DD., F.R.A.S., <u>Romanism and the Reformation – From the Standpoint of Prophecy,</u> Blackwood, New Jersey; Old Fashioned Prophecy Magazine, 1967, p. 114.

Referring to the Pre-Reformation Interpreters, Dr. Guinness states the following on pages 123-124 of the aforementioned book:

It should be noted that *none of the Fathers held the futurist gap theory*, the theory that the book of Revelation *overleaps* nearly eighteen centuries of Christian history, *plunging at once into the distant future*, and devoting itself entirely to predicting the events of the last few years of this dispensation. As to the subject of antichrist, there was a universal agreement among them concerning the *general idea* of the prophecy, while there were differences as to details, these differences arising chiefly from the notion that the antichrist would be in some way *Jewish* as well as *Roman*. It is true they thought that the antichrist would be an *individual man*. Their early position sufficiently accounts for this. They had no conception and could have no conception of the true *nature and length* of the tremendous apostasy which was to set in upon the Christian Church. *They were not prophets*, and could not foresee that the Church was to remain nineteen centuries in the wilderness, and to pass through prolonged and bitter persecution under the succession of nominally Christian but apostate rulers, filling the place of the ancient Caesars and emulating their antichristian deeds.[3]

3. H. Grattan Guinness, DD., F.R.A.S., Romanism and the Reformation – From the Standpoint of Prophecy, Blackwood, New Jersey; Old Fashioned Prophecy Magazine, 1967, pp. 123-124

The Origin of Futurism

So why, when and how did Futurism creep into early church doctrine? When this interpretation of prophecy began should be of particular interest to all schools of prophetic interpretation. Dr. Guinness throws open the door of enlightenment to that dubious honor with this revealing bit of history:

> We shall show that the futurist school of interpretation, on the contrary, is chiefly represented by teachers belonging to the Church of Rome; that the popes, cardinals, bishops, and priests of that apostate Church are all futurists, and that the futurist interpretation is one of the chief pillars of Romanism. [4]

> The former, or futurist system of interpreting the prophecies is now held, strange to say, by many Protestants, but it was first invented by the Jesuit Ribera, at the end of the sixteenth century, to relieve the Papacy from the terrible stigma cast upon it by the Protestant interpretation. This interpretation was so evidently the true and intended one, that the adherents of the Papacy felt its edge must, at any cost, be turned or blunted. If the Papacy were the predicted antichirst, as Protestants asserted, there was an end of the question, and separation from it became an imperative duty. [5]

> First, note the fact that Rome's reply to the Reformation in the 16th century *included an answer to the prophetic teachings of the Reformers.* Through the Jesuits *Ribera* and *Bellarmine*, Rome put forth her *futurist* interpretation of prophecy. Ribera was a Jesuit priest of Salamanca.

4. H. Grattan Guinness, DD., F.R.A.S., Romanism and the Reformation – From the Standpoint of Prophecy, Blackwood, New Jersey; Old Fashioned Prophecy Magazine, 1967, p. 114.
5. Ibid., p. 113

7

In 1585 he published a commentary on the Apocalypse, denying the application of the prophecies concerning antichrist to the existing Church of Rome. He was followed by *Cardinal Bellarmine*, a nephew of Pope Marcellus II, who was born in Tuscany in 1542, and died in Rome in 1621. Bellarmine was not only a man of great learning, but the most powerful controversialist in defence [sic] of Popery that the Roman Church ever produced." Clement VIII used these remarkable words on his nomination: "We choose him, because the Church of God does not possess his equal in learning." Bellarmine, like Ribera, advocated the futurist interpretation of prophecy. He taught that antichrist would be one particular man, that he would be a Jew, that he would be preceded by the reappearance of the literal Enoch and Elias, that he would rebuild the Jewish temple at Jerusalem, compel circumcision, abolish the Christian sacraments, abolish every other form of religion, would manifestly and avowedly deny Christ, would assume to be Christ, and would be received by the Jews as their Messiah, would pretend to be God, would make a literal image speak, would feign himself dead and rise again, and would conquer the whole world – Christian, Mohammedan, and heathen; and all this *in the space of three and a half years*. He insisted that the prophecies of Daniel, Paul, and John, with reference to the antichrist, *had no application whatever to the Papal power.* [6]

6. H. Grattan Guinness, DD., F.R.A.S., <u>Romanism and the Reformation – From the Standpoint of Prophecy,</u> Blackwood, New Jersey; Old Fashioned Prophecy Magazine, 1967, pp. 164-165.

There were only two alternatives. If the antichrist were not a present power, he must be either a past or a future one. Some writers asserted that the predictions pointed back to Nero. [This became the Preterist view] This did not take into account the obvious fact that the anti-Christian power predicted was to succeed the fall of the Caesars, and develop among the Gothic nations. The other alternative became therefore the popular one with Papists. Antichrist was future, so Ribera and Bossuet and others taught. An individual man was intended, not a dynasty; the duration of his power would not be for twelve and a half centuries, but only three and a half years; he would be a Jew, and sit in a Jewish temple. Speculation about the future took the place of study of the past and present, and careful comparison of the facts of history with the predictions of prophecy. This related, so it was asserted, not to the main course of the history of the Church, but only to the few closing years of her history. . .[7]

In another of his books, *The Approaching End of the Age*, Dr. Guinness sheds further light on the origins of Futurism:

The third or FUTURIST view, is that which teaches that the prophetic visions of Revelation, from chapters iv to xix, prefigure events *still wholly future* and not to take place, till just at the close of this dispensation. . . .

In its present form however it may be said to have originated at the end of the sixteenth century, with the Jesuit Ribera, who, moved like Alcazar, to relieve the Papacy from the terrible stigma cast upon it by the

7. H. Grattan Guinness, DD., F.R.A.S., <u>Romanism and the Reformation – From the Standpoint of Prophecy</u>, Blackwood, New Jersey; Old Fashioned Prophecy Magazine, 1967, p. 113

Protestant interpretation, tried to do so, by referring those prophecies to the distant future, instead of like Alcazar to the distant past. For a considerable period this view was confined to Romanists, and was refuted by several masterly Protestant works. But of late years, since the commencement of this century, it has sprung up afresh, and sprung up strange to say among Protestants. It was revived by such writers as the two Maitlands, Burgh, Tyso, Dr. Dodd, the leaders of the "Brethren" generally, and by some Puseyite expositors also . . .[8]

Another accomplished author and church historian who has written extensively on prophecy is Leroy Edwin Froom. In his book *The Prophetic Faith of Our Fathers*, Vol. II, he brings to light some startling bits of history:

As to Futurism, for some three centuries this view was virtually confined to Romanists, and was refuted by several masterly Protestant works. But early in the nineteenth century it sprang forth afresh, this time among Protestants – Samuel R. Maitland, William Burgh, J. H. Todd, and more recently it has been adopted by most Fundamentalists. In 1826 Maitland revived Ribera's Futurist interpretation in England. The Plymouth Brethren, organized in 1830 by John Nelson Darby, at Dublin and Plymouth, also laid hold on Maitland's interpretation. And when the High-Church Oxford Movement (1833-1845) gained ascendancy in Britain, it rejected the Protestant Historical School of interpretation and generally adopted Futurism, though some among them swung to Preterism. Bursting into full flame in 1833, it seized upon Maitland's interpretation as

---

8. H. Grattan Guinness, DD., F.R.A.S.,The Approaching End of the Age, London: Hodder and Stoughton, 1878, p. 95.

an argument in favor of reunion with Rome. German rationalism, on the other hand, increasingly flouted prophecy and prediction. Thus the Jesuit schemes of counter-interpretation were more successful than their authors had ever dared anticipate. [9]

Tanner expresses the tragedy of modern Protestantism thus playing into the hands of Romanism:

> It is a matter for deep regret that those who hold and advocate the Futurist system at the present day, Protestants as they are for the most part, are thus really playing into the hands of Rome, and helping to screen the Papacy from detection as the Antichrist. It has been well said that "Futurism tends to obliterate the brand put by the Holy Spirit upon Popery." More especially is this to be deplored at a time when the Papal Antichrist seems to be making an expiring effort to regain his former hold on men's minds. [10]

Thus, Guinness and others have opened the pages of history to reveal the origins of Futurist thinking. However, Romanism did not consider the Futurist interpretation of prophecy sufficient to lay all questions and objections to rest. There had to be another school of interpretation to answer those objects while simultaneously removing the Papacy from the Reformers' glare.

---

9. Edwin L. Froom, <u>The Prophetic Faith of Our Fathers</u>, Washington, D.C.: Review and Herald Publishing Association, 1948, Vol II, p. 511

10. Joseph Tanner, <u>Daniel and the Revelation</u>, London: Hodder and Stoughton, 1898, p. 17 quoted by Leroy E. Froom, <u>The Prophetic Faith of our Fathers</u>, Washington: Review and Herald Publishing Association, Vol. II, 1948, p. 511

The Papal Origins of Preterism

To lay further questions and objections to rest, another school of interpretation was developed. So just how and when did the Preterist school of prophetic interpretation begin? Dr. Guinness in his book *The Approaching End of the Age* answers that thought-provoking question with this observation:

> The first or PRETERIST scheme, considers these prophecies to have been fulfilled in the downfall of the Jewish nation and the old Roman Empire, limiting their range thus to the first six centuries of the Christian era, and making Nero Antichrist.

> This scheme originated with the Jesuit Alcazar toward the end of the sixteenth century; it has been held and taught under various modifications by Grotuis, Hammond, Bossuet, Eichhorn and other German commentators, Moses Stuart, and Dr. Davidson. **It has few supporters now** [Emphasis added], and need not be described more at length. [11]

Notice that Dr. Guinness mentions that Preterism had few supporters in 1887. However, today it is enjoying resurgence and is the view held by many of the Reformed faith. Those of the Preterist school of interpretation should take special note of Dr. Guinness' statement taken from page 113 of *Romanism and the Reformation:*

> Some writers asserted that the predictions pointed back to Nero. This did not take into account the obvious fact that the antichrist power predicted was to **succeed the fall**

11. H. Grattan Guinness, DD., F.R.A.S.,The Approaching End of the Age, London: Hodder and Stoughton, 1878, p. 93

of the Caesars, and develop among the Gothic nations.
[Emphasis added]. [12]

Leroy Froom in his book *The Prophetic Faith of Our Fathers*,
Vol. II confirms the foregoing facts of history:

> Rome's answer to the Protestant Reformation was two
> fold, though actually conflicting and contradictory.
> Through the Jesuits RIBERA, of Salamanca, Spain, and
> BELLARMINE, of Rome, the Papacy put forth her
> Futurist interpretation. And through Alcazar, Spanish
> Jesuit of Seville, she advanced almost simultaneously the
> conflicting Preterist interpretation. These were designed
> to meet and overwhelm the Historical interpretation of
> the Protestants. Though mutually exclusive, either Jesuit
> alternative suited the great objective equally well, as both
> thrust aside the application of the prophecies from the
> existing Church of Rome. The one accomplished it by
> making prophecy stop altogether short of Papal Rome's
> career. The other achieved it by making it overleap the
> immense era of Papal dominance, crowding Antichrist
> into a small fragment of time in the still distant future, just
> before the great consummation. It is consequently often
> called the gap theory. . .

Concerning the two alternatives, presented by Ribera and
Alcazar, consigning Antichrist either to the remote past or future,
Joseph Tanner, the Protestant writer, gives this record:

---

12. H. Grattan Guinness, DD., F.R.A.S., Romanism and the Reformation – From the Standpoint
of Prophecy, Blackwood, New Jersey; Old Fashioned Prophecy Magazine, 1967, p. 113

Accordingly, toward the close of the century of the Reformation, two of her most learned doctors set themselves to the task, each endeavoring by different means to accomplish the same end, namely, that of diverting men's minds from perceiving the fulfilment [sic] of the prophecies of the Antichirst in the Papal system. The Jesuit Alcasar devoted himself to bring into prominence the *Preterist* method of interpretation, which we have already briefly noticed, and thus endeavored to show that the prophecies of Antichrist were fulfilled before the Popes ever ruled at Rome, and therefore could not apply to the Papacy. On the other hand the Jesuit Ribera tried to set aside the application of these prophecies to the Papal Power by bringing out the *Futurist* system, which asserts that these prophecies refer properly not to the career of the Papacy, but to that of some future supernatural individual, who is yet to appear, and to continue in power for three and a half years. Thus, as Alford says, the Jesuit Ribera, about A.D. 1580, may be regarded as the Founder of the Futurist system in modern times.

E.B. Elliott states precisely the same fact, only assigning slightly different dates; and many others such as Dr. Candish, of Edinburgh, also support the charges. Thus the fact is established.[13]

Rev. E. B. Elliott, quoted by Froom in the preceding paragraph, is that great English scholar from Cambridge University. In his

---

13. Joseph Tanner, Daniel and the Revelation, London: Hodder and Stoughton, 1898, pp. 16, 17 quoted by Rev, E. B. Elliott, A.M. Horae Apocalypticae; or A Commentary on the Apocalypse, London: Seeley, Jackosn, and Halliday, 1862, Vol. 4, 5th Edition, pp. 480-485 as quoted by Edwin L. Froom, The Prophetic Faith of Our Fathers, Washington: Review and Herald Publishing Association, Vol. II, 1948, p. 486-488.

four volume literary masterpiece, *Horae Apocalypticae; or A Commentary on the Apocalypse, Critical and Historical*, Elliott supports the evidence thus far that both Preterist and Futurist interpretations of prophecy originated with Rome:

It was stated at the conclusion of my *Sketch of the History of Apocalyptic Interpretation,* that there are at present *two,* and but two, grand general *counter-Schemes* to what may be called the *historic Protestant* view of the Apocalypse: that view which regards the prophecy as a prefiguration of the great events that were to happen in the Church, and the world connected with it, from St. John's time to the consummation; including specially the establishment of the Popedom, and reign of Papal Rome, as in some way or other the fulfilment [sic] of the types of the Apocalyptic Beast and Babylon. The *first* of these two counter-Schemes is the *Praeterists',* which would have the prophecy stop altogether short of the Popedom, explaining it of the catastrophes, one or both, of the *Jewish Nation* and *Pagan Rome*; and of which there are two sufficiently distinct varieties: the *second* the Futurists'; which in its original form would have it all shoot over the head of the Popedom into times yet future; and refer simply to the events that are immediately to precede, or to accompany, Christ's second Advent; or, in its various modified forms, have them for its chief subject. I shall in this second Part of my Appendix proceed successively to examine these two, or rather four, anti-Protestant counter-Schemes; and show, if I mistake not, the palpable untenableness alike of one and all. Which done, it may perhaps be well, from respect to his venerated name, to add an examination of the late Dr. Arnold's general prophetic counter-*theory*. This, together with a notice of certain recent counter-views on the Millennium, will complete our review of counter-prophetic Schemes.

Now with regard to the *Praeterist Scheme*, on the review of which we are first to enter, it may be remembered that I stated it to have had its origin with the Jesuit Alcasar, and that it was subsequently, and after *Grotius'* and *Hammond's* prior adoption of it, adopted and improved by *Bossuet,* the great Papal champion, under *one* form and modification; then afterwards, under *another* modification, by *Hernnschneider*, *Eichhorn*, and others of the **German critical and generally infidel school of the last half-century** [Emphasis added]; followed in our own era by *Heinrichs*, and by *Moses Stuart* of the United States of America. The two modifications appear to have arisen mainly out of the differences of date assigned to the Apocalypse; whether about the end of Nero's reign or Domitian's. I shall, I think, pretty well exhaust whatever can be thought to call for examination in the system in considering separately, first the *Neronic*, or favourite *German* form and modification of the Praeterist Scheme, as propounded by *Eichhorn, Hug, Heinrichs,* and *Moses Stuart;* secondly *Bossuet's* Domitianic form, the one most generally approved, I believe, by Roman Catholics. [14]

Froom makes a significant observation in the following treatise, though he did not draw overt attention to it, that it was the **rationalists** who revived and advanced the Preterist theory:

---

14. Rev, E. B. Elliott, A.M. Horae Apocalypticae; or A Commentary on the Apocalypse, London: Seeley, Jackosn, and Halliday, 1862, , Appendix, Part II, Vol. 4, pp. 564-565

First, as to Preterism's penetrations into Protestantism, we may note that in 1791 J.G. Eichhorn (1752-1827), the noted German rationalist, revived and republished Alcazar's Preterist interpretation. Soon he was joined by other rationalist scholars, such as G.H.A. Ewald (1803-1875), G.C.F. Lucke (1791-1855), W.M.L. De Wette (1780-1849), Franz Delitsch (1813-1890), and Julius Wellhausen (1844-1918). And since 1830 numerous British and American scholars have followed Eichhorn. In 1830 Prof. Samuel Lee of Cambridge, likewise injected Bossuet's Preterist interpretation into the discussion. Prof. Moses Stuart, of Andover (1780-1852), introduced Preterism into the United States about 1842, and Dr. Samuel Davidson reiterated it in England in 1844. These, and many others, all contended with the Papacy that nothing beyond the destruction of pagan Rome and Judaism was intended by the prophecies concerning Antichrist in the Apocalypse.[15]

While Froom identifies those who advanced Preterism as rationalists, it was Elliott who was even more accurate in his description of them. Remember his words:

". . .then afterwards, under another modification, by Hernnschneider, Eichhorn, and others of German critical and generally infidel school of the last half-century followed in our own era by Heinrichs, and by Moses Stuart of the United States of America."

Summation

It is argued that the revelations of Guinness, Tanner, Elliott, Froom, and others are simply anti-Catholic vilification and of no

---

15. Leroy E. Froom, The Prophectic Faith of Our Fathers, Washington:Reciew and Herald Publishing Association, 1948, Vol II, p. 510.

historical accuracy. On the contrary, Roman Catholics as well as Protestants agree as to the origin of these interpretations. The Roman Catholic writer G.S. Hitchcock writes:

> The Futuristic School, founded by the Jesuit Ribera in 1591, looks for Antichrist, Babylon and a rebuilt temple in Jerusalem, at the end of the Christian Dispensation. The Praeterist School, founded by Jesuit Alcasar in 1614, explains the Revelation by the Fall of Jerusalem, or by the fall of Pagan Rome in 410 A.D. [16]

This Roman Catholic confirmation of the origins of Futurism and Preterism validates the writings of Froom, Elliott, Guinness and others.

To answer the question posed at the beginning of this booklet concerning the origin of the Futurist and Preterist views of prophecy, all of the writers quoted are in agreement: Rome is guilty.

While the original question has been answered, it should be pointed out that at this late date in history the political and spiritual ramifications from either of these errors should be carefully considered by all. The most obvious one is the slow drift back to Rome we see in many of our churches and para-church groups.

For these errors to have grown to the extent seen today it would appear a substantial segment of our Protestant ministers and theologians have neglected a careful and thorough study of church history and the prophetic Word. While none of us has all knowledge, and cherished dogmas are difficult

---

16. George S. Hitchcock, <u>The Beasts and the Little Horn</u>, London, Catholic Truth Society Publications, 1911, p. 7.

to abandon, it behooves us to listen to the Apostle Paul's words of commendation about the Church at Berea:

Acts 17:10-11

"And the brethren immediately sent away Paul and Silas by night unto Berea: who coming thither went into the synagogue of the Jews. These were more noble than those in Thessalonica, in that they received the word with all readiness of mind, and searched the scriptures daily, whether those things were so."

THE DEVELOPMENT OF PRETERISM
AND ITS INTERPRETATION OF THE SECOND
COMING OF CHRIST

SECTION TWO

In addition to the review of the origin of Preterism and Futurism, a few pages should be penned giving clear Scriptural authority as to why Preterism, especially, is in error. This will be done, but first a few thoughts as background material.

It should be remembered that all viewpoints, be they Preterist, Futurist or Historicist, have the same Rulebook to play by – the Holy Bible, all sixty-six books. New manuscripts by Paul or John have not surfaced in Egypt, nor has the Vatican brought forth additional writings by Peter. The problem is how one interprets the existing Scriptures that have been given to us by God Himself.

While the writers previously quoted agreed that Rome was responsible for the present-day teaching that all prophecy found in John's Book of Revelation was fulfilled in 70 AD, or at the fall of Pagan Rome, church history reveals traces of this error beginning in the early church age.

Actually, the Preterist of today can trace some of their dogmas back to the first and second centuries AD, so the revival of Preterism is nothing new. As Solomon said, *". . .There is no new thing under the sun"* (Ecclesiastes 1:9).

The Seeds are Planted

So how and when were the seeds of Preterism planted?

As those Apostles and disciples who knew and spoke with Christ after His resurrection began dying off, and Christ had not returned as promised, the thought arose among some of the ecclesiastical leaders in the early centuries that perhaps they had misunderstood. Could there be another explanation as to why He had not returned? While the early church fathers as a whole stood fast in the original teaching, there were some who were disappointed and open to further speculation and theory.

One of those early church fathers was Origen (185-254 AD) who, along with others of the Alexandrian School of Theology, was prone to spiritualizing Scripture. As to Jesus' Second coming it was spiritual and already past. Some equated His coming with Pentecost, others to the destruction of Jerusalem in 70 AD.

By the fourth century AD, when it was reported that Constantine had converted to Christianity, it became popular to be a Christian. Constantine made Christianity the state religion, which brought about the marriage of church and state.

As the state church increased in size, power and wealth, the teachings of Christ and the apostles and disciples faded into the background. It began to teach that surely Christ had already come, and the church was the Kingdom. Who needed Paul's admonition in Titus 2:13: *"Looking for that blessed hope and the glorious appearing of the great God and our Savior Jesus Christ"?*

Centuries passed, and in the Middle Ages, when Rome was at its height of power, a literal coming of Jesus Christ would have been an embarrassment to the "Church." They were doing quite well, thank you! They controlled the ecclesiastical world as well as the political and had no need of Christ. They were already in the millennium, ruling and reigning with Christ. Why would they think otherwise? They had control of it all.

A Matter of Timing

As the reader may have noted, it was and still is a matter of timing. Man's timing was out of sync with God's eternal plan. The lack of understanding of God's timing has often led man into many blind alleys. Although Peter reminds us in II Peter 3:8 to *". . .be not ignorant of this one thing, that one day is with the Lord as a thousand years, and a thousand years as one day,"* it is difficult for we mortals to comprehend that God does not live in time as we do.

The problem with timing occurs not only with the Second Coming, but also with all historical events in Scripture. Example: the manifestation of the Kingdom. Most Christians believe in the Kingdom, but is it spiritual, literal, or both? Is it present now or to be set up at Christ's Second Coming? This small booklet will not attempt to examine the many answers that individuals give to those questions, but it will provide those clues that exist within the Scriptures regarding the Second Coming.

Even in Paul's day, there were those who were off in their timing and understanding of the resurrection. Paul scourges Hymenaeus and Philetus with the following words:

II Timothy 2:17-18
"And their word will eat as doth a canker: of whom is Hymenaeus and Philetus; Who concerning the truth have erred, saying that the resurrection is past already; and overthrow the faith of some."

Preterism's Progressive Course

During the early centuries when the spiritualization of Scripture had secured a firm footing, other errors began to creep in. Error begets more error. Some of those errors that took hold in the church and the events that took place subsequent to those errors led progressively to a state church. A few of these errors and events are shown below:

Errors:

Christ returned spiritually, either at Pentecost or at 70 AD at the destruction of Jerusalem; therefore, we must be in the Kingdom now. The Church *is* the Kingdom.

The promises made to Israel in the Old Testament are of a spiritual nature, therefore, they find their fulfillment in the "church."

The millennium has arrived; therefore, we are ruling and reigning with Christ.

Events:

Once-pagan ruler, Constantine, converted to Christianity and declared Christianity to be the state religion.

The church and state married, and as time passed, "the church" assumed more and more power and wealth.

This state church began teaching the foregoing spiritual interpretation as truth, and they believed it was their duty to teach these precepts to all nations and to stamp out all error and unbelief wherever found.

Any knowledgeable Christian should at once recognize these progressive steps as the history of the Roman Catholic Church.

An in-depth look at church and secular history will reveal the inevitability that any church group or organization that follows these progressive steps and erroneous precepts will eventually terminate in a state or world church. While all Christians earnestly yearn for God's Kingdom to rule the earth, knowledgeable Christians recognize that until the King returns and those who will rule with Him are incorruptible, there can be no righteous ruling and reigning.

It is of interest that the early church had one Sword – the Sword of the Spirit – and did very well. In less than 300 years, by prayer, preaching, teaching and witnessing, they had won so much of the populous to Christ – from slave and peasant to those of Caesar's household – that the pagan state wanted to join them. Unfortunately, the state churches, by whatever name, attempted to use two swords: the Sword of the Spirit plus the sword of the magistrate. History would seem to indicate that this combination is not nearly as effective *spiritually* as those who used but the one Sword – the Sword of the Spirit.

CHRIST'S SECOND COMING
AND
UNFULFILLED PROPHECIES

A significant error, and the Scriptural responses to that error, are found below.

Some Preterists believe that although Christ did come at Pentecost (33 AD) and 70 AD, He will make a final appearance at the end of the world (age). Others strongly maintain that His second appearance was a spiritual one in 70 AD and that is the end of it.

Please note that the following Scriptures are very clear and not limited to one or two obscure verses that might easily be interpreted as one wished. The authors are of the highest caliber who were honest, godly men filled with the Holy Spirit – Luke, John and Paul. Please read carefully and prayerfully.

Acts 1:10-11
*"And while they looked stedfastly toward heaven as he went up, behold, two men stood by them in white apparel; Which also said, Ye men of Galilee, why stand ye gazing up into heaven? this same Jesus, which is taken up from you into heaven, **shall so come in like manner as ye have seen him go into heaven.**"*

Titus 2:13
"Looking for that blessed hope, and the glorious appearing of the great God and our Saviour Jesus Christ;"

II Timothy 2:15-18

*"**Study to shew thyself approved unto God**, a workman that needeth not to be ashamed, rightly dividing the word of truth. **But shun profane and vain babblings**: for they will increase unto more ungodliness. **And their word will eat as doth a canker: of whom is Hymenaeus and Philetus; Who concerning the truth have erred, saying that the resurrection is past already; and overthrow the faith of some."***

Paul wrote these words to Timothy in late 67 AD or early 68 AD. For those who believe that Christ returned at Pentecost (approximately 33 AD) and thus that the resurrection has occurred, Paul has laid their claims to rest. For those who believe He secretly returned at 70 AD, see Revelation 20:4-6 at the end of these passages.

John 14:3

"And if I go and prepare a place for you, I will come again, and receive you unto myself; that where I am, there ye may be also."

I John 3:2

*"Beloved, now are we the sons of God, and it doth not yet appear what we shall be: **but we know that, when he shall appear, we shall be like him;** for we shall see him as he is."*

Do we <u>see</u> Him as He is today? Are <u>we</u> like Him? No. . .

I Thessalonians 1:10

"And to wait for his Son from heaven, whom he raised from the dead, even Jesus, which delivered us from the wrath to come."

I Thessalonians 4:13-17

*"But I would not have you to be ignorant, brethren, concerning them which are asleep, that ye sorrow not, even as others which have no hope. **For if we believe that Jesus died and rose again, even so them also which sleep in Jesus will God bring with him**. For this we say unto you by the word of the Lord, that we which are alive and remain unto the coming of the Lord shall not prevent them which are asleep. **For the Lord himself shall descend from heaven with a shout, with the voice of the archangel, and with the trump of God: and the dead in Christ shall rise first: Then we which are alive and remain shall be caught up together with them in the clouds, to meet the Lord in the air:** and so shall we ever be with the Lord."*

It should be an obvious fact that Jesus' Second Coming and the resurrection of the righteous occur as one event. The resurrection is a result of His coming.

II Peter 3:3-4

*"Knowing this first, that **there shall come in the last days scoffers**, walking after their own lusts, And saying, Where is the promise of his coming? for since the fathers fell asleep, all things continue as they were from the beginning of the creation."*

Revelation 20:4-6

*"And I saw thrones, and they sat upon them, and judgment was given unto them: and I saw the souls of them that were beheaded for the witness of Jesus, and for the word of God, and which had not worshipped the beast, neither his image, neither had received his mark upon their foreheads, or in their hands; **and they lived and reigned with Christ a thousand years.** But the rest of the dead lived not again*

until the thousand years were finished. This is the first resurrection. **Blessed and holy is he that hath part in the first resurrection: on such the second death hath no power, but they shall be priests of God and of Christ, and shall reign with him a thousand years.***"*

II Thessalonians 1:7-10
"And to you who are troubled rest with us, when the Lord Jesus shall be revealed from heaven with his mighty angels, *In flaming fire taking vengeance on them that know not God, and that obey not the gospel of our Lord Jesus Christ: Who shall be punished with everlasting destruction from the presence of the Lord, and from the glory of his power; When he shall come to be glorified in his saints, and to be admired in all them that believe (because our testimony among you was believed) in that day."*

Has history *ever* recorded this awesome event?

Hebrews 9:27-28
"And as it is appointed unto men once to die, but after this the judgment: So Christ was once offered to bear the sins of many; **and unto them that look for him shall he appear the second time without sin unto salvation."**

Philippians 3:20-21
"For our conversation is in heaven; **from whence also we look for the Saviour, the Lord Jesus Christ: Who shall change our vile body, that it may be fashioned like unto his glorious body,** *according to the working whereby he is able even to subdue all things unto himself."*

Our bodies continue to age daily; they are not perfect; they are subject to decay (corruption); they become ill; they have not been fashioned like unto His glorious body because He has not yet returned, and we have not been resurrected or changed.

The Modernists, Rationalists and, as Dr. Elliott describes them, "those of the infidel school," are fond of spiritualizing the following verses from Luke, Chapter 1. Surely, no Christian would do so. However, just as absurd would be an attempt to read verses 30-31 literally yet spiritualize verses 32-33.

Luke 1:30-33
*"And the angel said unto her, Fear not, Mary: for thou hast found favour with God. And, behold, thou shalt conceive in thy womb, and bring forth a son, and shalt call his name JESUS. **He shall be great, and shall be called the Son of the Highest: and the Lord God shall give unto him the throne of his father David: And he shall reign over the house of Jacob for ever; and of his kingdom there shall be no end."***

Again, it is a matter of timing. The Christ was conceived and brought forth. Now, we await His return, for God to give Him the throne of David, and for Him to reign over His Kingdom on earth as promised.

To you who have read these Scriptures pertaining to the Second coming of Christ, a question: "How readest thou?"

Historicists have been forced to the conclusion that those who can read these Scriptures and maintain they do not mean what they clearly state, but need changing, twisting, or spiritualizing, must have come to the Bible with preconceived conclusions and are desperately looking for Scriptures to hang them on.

UNFULFILLED PROPHECY
AS OF 70 AD

SECTION THREE

According to Preterism, all prophecy given must have found fulfillment during the period between its origin and 70 AD, and some Preterists extend that to the fall of Pagan Rome in 410 AD.

Again, timing is the issue. Historicists believe many prophecies have not been fulfilled or were fulfilled after 410 AD. Read the following carefully and prayerfully using your common sense.

The prophecy chosen for this little booklet is the well-known story found in Daniel 2 of Babylonian King Nebuchadnezzar and his dream of a great image.

Daniel 2:31-35

"Thou, O king, sawest, and behold a great image. This great image, whose brightness was excellent, stood before thee; and the form thereof was terrible. This image's head was of fine gold, his breast and his arms of silver, his belly and his thighs of brass, His legs of iron, his feet part of iron and part of clay. Thou sawest till that a stone was cut out without hands, which smote the image upon his feet that were of iron and clay, and brake them to pieces. Then was the iron, the clay, the brass, the silver, and the gold, broken to pieces together, and became like the chaff of the summer threshing floors; and the wind carried them away,

that no place was found for them: and the stone that smote the image became a great mountain, and filled the whole earth.*"

Daniel interprets the vision of the King in Chapter 2.

Daniel 2:36-43

"This is the dream; and we will tell the interpretation thereof before the king. Thou, O king, art a king of kings: for the God of heaven hath given thee a kingdom, power, and strength, and glory. And wheresoever the children of men dwell, the beasts of the field and the fowls of the heaven hath he given into thine hand, and hath made thee ruler over them all. Thou art this head of gold. And after thee shall arise another kingdom inferior to thee, and another third kingdom of brass, which shall bear rule over all the earth. And the fourth kingdom shall be strong as iron: forasmuch as iron breaketh in pieces and subdueth all things: and as iron that breaketh all these, shall it break in pieces and bruise. And whereas thou sawest the feet and toes, part of potters' clay, and part of iron, the kingdom shall be divided; but there shall be in it of the strength of the iron, forasmuch as thou sawest the iron mixed with miry clay. And as the toes of the feet were part of iron, and part of clay, so the kingdom shall be partly strong, and partly broken. And whereas thou sawest iron mixed with miry clay, they shall mingle themselves with the seed of men: but they shall not cleave one to another, even as iron is not mixed with clay."

In Daniel Chapter 7, Daniel had a dream which corresponds to Nebuchadnezzar's dream in Chapter 2, only it is from God's viewpoint.

Daniel 7:2-7

"Daniel spake and said, I saw in my vision by night, and, behold, the four winds of the heaven strove upon the great sea. And four great beasts came up from the sea, diverse one from another. The first was like a lion, and had eagle's wings: I beheld till the wings thereof were plucked, and it was lifted up from the earth, and made stand upon the feet as a man, and a man's heart was given to it. And behold another beast, a second, like to a bear, and it raised up itself on one side, and it had three ribs in the mouth of it between the teeth of it: and they said thus unto it, Arise, devour much flesh. After this I beheld, and lo another, like a leopard, which had upon the back of it four wings of a fowl; the beast had also four heads; and dominion was given to it. After this I saw in the night visions, and behold a fourth beast, dreadful and terrible, and strong exceedingly; and it had great iron teeth: it devoured and brake in pieces, and stamped the residue with the feet of it: and it was diverse from all the beasts that were before it; and it had ten horns."

Daniel was told the interpretation in verses 16-27:

Daniel 7:15-27

"I Daniel was grieved in my spirit in the midst of my body, and the visions of my head troubled me. I came near unto one of them that stood by, and asked him the truth of all this. So he told me, and made me know the interpretation of the things. These great beasts, which are four, are four kings, which shall arise out of the earth. But the saints of the most High shall take the kingdom, and possess the kingdom for ever, even for ever and ever. Then I would know the truth of the fourth beast, which was diverse from all the others,

exceeding dreadful, whose teeth were of iron, and his nails of brass; which devoured, brake in pieces, and stamped the residue with his feet; And of the ten horns that were in his head, and of the other which came up, and before whom three fell; even of that horn that had eyes, and a mouth that spake very great things, whose look was more stout than his fellows. I beheld, and the same horn made war with the saints, and prevailed against them; Until the Ancient of days came, and judgment was given to the saints of the most High; and the time came that the saints possessed the kingdom. Thus he said, The fourth beast shall be the fourth kingdom upon earth, which shall be diverse from all kingdoms, and shall devour the whole earth, and shall tread it down, and break it in pieces. And the ten horns out of this kingdom are ten kings that shall arise: and another shall rise after them; and he shall be diverse from the first, and he shall subdue three kings. And he shall speak great words against the most High, and shall wear out the saints of the most High, and think to change times and laws: and they shall be given into his hand until a time and times and the dividing of time. But the judgment shall sit, and they shall take away his dominion, to consume and to destroy it unto the end. And the kingdom and dominion, and the greatness of the kingdom under the whole heaven, shall be given to the people of the saints of the most High, whose kingdom is an everlasting kingdom, and all dominions shall serve and obey him."

All seems in agreement; the four parts of the image and the four beasts picture the same four kingdoms beginning with Babylon, then Medo-Persia, Greece and Rome.

If the story ended with the iron legs of the image and the terrible beast with the iron teeth from the sea, it would simplify matters considerably. However, it does not end there. The iron legs extend into two feet having ten toes, and those feet and toes are composed of iron mixed with clay. The iron legs represent the old Pagan Rome, but the feet and toes of iron mixed with clay represent the old paganism which became mixed with Papal Rome. For over one thousand years, no king ruled in the European nations (an average of ten) who was not under the approval and control of the Pope of Rome.

The timing is clear, as the pagan Roman Empire fell, another power rose to take its place – Ecclesiastical Rome who ruled the ten individual nations that formed out of the European continent. This happened well after the destruction of Jerusalem in 70 AD or even the fall of Pagan Rome in 410 AD.

The vision given to Daniel in Chapter 7 tells the same story in a different form. This beast is not content to be an ordinary terrible beast. It had the same number of appendages, but they were horns, not toes. As verse 24 advises: "and the ten horns *out of this kingdom* are ten kings that should arise."

Obviously, to come out of the original kingdom – Pagan Rome – it had to be *subsequent in time* to that old Roman Empire. What did emerge from the old Roman Empire? Papal Rome.

It should be of great interest that the Apostle John saw this same dreadful beast with its ten horns. He wrote of it in Revelation, Chapters 12 and 13.

Revelation 12:3-4
"And there appeared another wonder in heaven; and behold a great red dragon, having seven heads and ten horns, and seven crowns upon his heads. And his tail drew the third part of the stars of heaven, and did cast them to

*the earth: and the dragon stood before the woman which
was ready to be delivered, for to devour her child as soon
as it was born."*

Revelation 13:1
*"And I stood upon the sand of the sea, and saw a beast rise
up out of the sea, having seven heads and ten horns, and
upon his horns ten crowns, and upon his heads the name
of blasphemy."*

It is safe to assume that this beast is the same in both instances,
but no doubt you have noted one difference. The dragon in
Chapter 12 had *seven crowns upon his heads* while the beast in
Chapter 13 had *the ten crowns upon his horns.*

Revelation 17:9
*"And here is the mind which hath wisdom. The seven heads
are seven mountains, on which the woman sitteth."*

These two chapters clearly portray the difference in timing we
are so interested in. Chapter 12 shows seven crowns (power,
authority, forms of government) upon his heads – the seven
mountains upon which Rome was built. Chapter 13 moves the
ten crowns to his horns (nations, kingdoms) into which Pagan
Rome was divided into at its fall.

Obviously, the crowns of power and authority could not be
placed on the horns (nations) until the nations were formed. This
took place during the rise of Papal Rome.

As Dr. Guinness so clearly observed:

Some writers asserted that the predictions pointed back to
Nero; this did not take into account the obvious fact that

the antichrist power predicted was to succeed the fall of the Caesars, and develop among the Gothic nations."[17]

These brief remarks referring to Daniel, Chapters 2 and 7, plus Revelation 12 and 13, are for the purpose of calling attention to the timing of the prophecies, not to a theological discussion of them.

The Historicists expect those of Rome to propagate the Preterist theory. However, for Protestant Christians, with a Bible in one hand and a history book in the other, to be taken in by this error is almost unbelievable.

17. H. Grattan Guinness, DD., F.R.A.S., Romanism and the Reformation – From the Standpoint of Prophecy, Blackwood, New Jersey; Old Fashioned Prophecy Magazine, 1967, p. 113

MISUNDERSTANDING AND MISAPPLICATION OF SCRIPTURE

The misunderstanding that all prophecy has been fulfilled leaves much to be desired. The Jews in Jerusalem misunderstood Christ's First Coming and the Preterists misunderstand His Second Coming.

Most Historicists find it ludicrous to believe that the Holy Spirit inspired the writers of Matthew 24 and Luke 21, and directed the Apostle John to write the Book of Revelation simply to prophesy of the coming destruction of Jerusalem, the holocaust perpetrated against the Southern Kingdom of Judah, and to alert the few thousand new Christians in the area to flee when the Roman Legions appeared on the scene. This teaching omits any word of the upcoming scourge that was to descend upon the Christian Church throughout Europe during the ensuing centuries. This is myopic in the extreme!

Yes, God did fulfill His Word: Jerusalem and the Temple were destroyed, and one million plus of the Southern Kingdom of Judah were slain, and tens of thousands of Jews were sold into slavery. For those with eyes to see and ears to hear, the Southern Kingdom was destroyed; the Temple sacrificial system was ended; the commandments contained in the ordinances had been fulfilled. As the Scripture states:

Hebrews 9:26
"For then must he often have suffered since the foundation of the world: but now once in the end of the world hath he appeared to put away sin by the sacrifice of himself."

All agree that the events in 70 AD were shocking and horrible, but there was another holocaust that would soon appear on the horizon. Church historians tell of 50-60 million Christians who were killed in the most heinous manner that demonic men could envision during the 1200-1300 years when Papal Rome held sway. To believe that God said nothing of this in Scripture is nonsense.

Protestants as a whole have but a vague idea of the terrible persecutions heaped upon the "nonconformists" by the Roman Catholic Church during the Middle Ages. These nonconforming groups went by a variety of names: Donatists, Anabaptists, Waldenses, etc. It is of interest to note that these particular groups actually came through the Reformation and not out of it.

As noted before, if one adds the number of martyrs in the nonconformist groups to the myriad of believers who perished in the Protestant churches that had formed or were forming, the number is staggering. Comparing the *one* million who died in 70 AD in Jerusalem to the *fifty* or *sixty* million who died during the reign of Papal Rome throughout Europe over a period of twelve to thirteen hundred centuries, makes the destruction of Jerusalem, the Temple and the number involved pale in comparison.

Another misunderstanding of prophecy relates to the timing and fruits of Christ's *Second* Coming. His *First* Coming is found in one of the most important and far-reaching prophecies in Scripture:

Genesis 3:15
> *"And I will put enmity between thee and the woman, and between thy seed and her seed; it shall bruise thy head, and thou shalt bruise his heel."*

The fulfillment of that prophecy was the birth, death and resurrection of the Lord Jesus Christ who will destroy the works of Satan and ultimately bring humanity and creation back into proper relationship with God. *It should be remembered that this prophecy took 4,000 years to come to pass.*

The religious leaders of Jesus' day misunderstood the entire event – confusing His First and Second Coming. They anticipated and eagerly awaited a Messianic rule of power and glory, but the First Coming, to remedy the sin question, was dismissed as unnecessary. Were they not the children of Abraham, Isaac and Jacob? Did they not have the Law of Moses? Did they not keep the Law? Their man interest was political: "Get those Romans off our backs."

First, they missed an important point in timing. For the Second Coming to materialize, the First Coming must occur, and be fulfilled. Secondly, they missed an important spiritual truth: for the political – earthly – problems to be addressed, spiritual qualifications had to first be met.

> **John 3:3, 7**
> *"Jesus answered and said unto him, Verily, verily, I say unto thee, Except a man be born again, he cannot see the kingdom of God.*
>
> *Marvel not that I said unto thee, Ye must be born again."*

Today, Christians have no problem with the First Coming or with its purpose.

Matthew 1:21
"And she shall bring forth a son, and thou shalt call his name JESUS: for he shall save his people from their sins."

However, the Preterists of today have problems with the Second Coming just as the religious leaders of Christ's day had with His First Coming. Some take the position that He has come spiritually, long ago. Others consider it their duty to bring in the anticipated Kingdom while they await Christ's subsequent return. To accomplish this, the nation must be taught to administer the Law of the Lord in all areas of government. It would seem considerable political clout would be needed to bring these results.

Speaking of politics, Peter's question to Jesus and our Lord's reply in Matthew 19, is most interesting:

Matthew 19:27-28
"Then answered Peter and said unto him, Behold, we have forsaken all, and followed thee; what shall we have therefore? And Jesus said unto them, Verily I say unto you, That ye which have followed me, in the regeneration when the Son of man shall sit in the throne of his glory, ye also shall sit upon twelve thrones, judging the twelve tribes of Israel."

You will notice that Jesus did not say, "Peter, one more year's study with me, and you men will be ready to take over positions of leadership in Jerusalem."

Timing is extremely important. *". . .in the regeneration when the Son of man shall sit in the throne of his glory."* This is the Second Coming when Jesus, among other things, will see that justice is administered throughout the earth. And, wonder of wonders, the Apostles, in resurrected, glorified bodies, will have a political position to judge Israel.

While we all long for, work for, pray for and vote for righteous government, as Christians we are painfully aware that we are sill in our Adamic bodies. We earnestly look forward to the day when *". . . this corruptible must put on incorruption, and this mortal must put on immortality"* (I Corinthians 15:53). This will happen when Christ truly returns, and we are *". . .raised a spiritual body"* (I Corinthians 15:44). Then, and only then, are we fit to rule and reign in God's literal kingdom.

As we contemplate these tremendous promises, we cry with the Apostle John, *"Even so, come, Lord Jesus"* (Revelation 22:20).

PART TWO

THE TRAGIC AFTERMATH OF FUTURISM
by Charles A. Jennings

For the last 175 years, the Futuristic prophetic viewpoint has been gaining prominence within evangelical Christianity. During that time, its influence has increased from a trickle to an overwhelming flood-tide in doctrinal statements and evangelistic preaching. The curricula of most Bible colleges and theological seminaries have totally ignored the prophetic viewpoints of our Protestant Reformation fathers and other great Bible scholars of the past. Instead, they have strictly adopted the viewpoint of prophecy which had its origin among the Jesuit priesthood of the Roman Catholic Church's counter-reformation. It was picked up by the Plymouth Brethren churches of Great Britain and then brought to the United States and widely promoted which influenced multiplied thousands of ministers and laymen alike.

Within the last seventy-five years or so, ever since the "fundamentalists" accepted Futurism, there has been a plethora of sermons and written material that has thoroughly convinced millions of Christians that it is the truth of God's Word. They are so thoroughly convinced that most are more than willing to break fellowship with other believers and even condemn them to the region of the eternally damned over any disagreement or denial of their belief. Very few other religious issues have created more modern Pharisees within the ranks of the body of Christ.

Many sincere saints have contacted this ministry and expressed their fear and apprehension to even mention in their church fellowships their doubts about the rapture. Some have even been excommunicated and considered as heretics. A classic case is a recent letter that we received from some truth-seeking trembling souls. They wrote: "My pastor says there is a rapture before the tribulation, and if I don't believe his way, I can leave the church. Please, please help me. I am very depressed and anxiety ridden, as is my wife. We are so scared of being kicked out of the church if we disagree with the pastor. Our nerves are a jumble every time we listen to him. He sends shivers up our spines. I want the truth! I want the truth! Signed _____ "

Within the last forty years with the rapid advance in technology, the distress among nations, social and cultural unrest, there has been a heightened interest in prophecy with an expectation that something big is about to happen. Prophecy "experts" have taken advantage of this social, political and religious climate to promote and even "cash in" on the prosperous prophecy market.

The shelves of most religious book stores are attractively arranged to catch the eye and the pocketbook of the innocent and naive Christian public. Most of this material is promoting Futuristic ideas such as a secret pre-tribulation rapture of the Church, the rise of a one-man Antichrist that makes a covenant with the Jews which he breaks after three and a half years, a seven year tribulation which is purported to be the seventieth week of Daniel, the rebuilding of the Jewish temple in Jerusalem and the reinstitution of the Old Testament animal sacrificial system.

The Definition of Futurism

Futurism is that distinctive religious interpretation of Bible prophecy, allegedly based upon the message of the angel Gabriel as recorded in Daniel 9:20-27. It places the fulfillment of the last nineteen chapters of the Book of Revelation into the future with its starting point at the rapture of the church and lasting for seven years. This seven year period is supposed to be the seventieth week of Daniel. The Futurists utilize other Scriptural passages throughout the Bible to support their theory, but mainly: Matthew 24, I Thessalonians 4:13-18 and others while interpreting all symbols in a literal sense.

The Development of Futurism

In order to properly understand the historical development of Futurism, one must first have a general knowledge of the religious climate of the times in which the Roman Catholic Church was most dominant in Europe. Many Bible students of the 13th and 14th centuries accepted the **"Historicist"** interpretation of prophecy. This included many teachers who were loyal to the Church of Rome. Many of that time who adhered to the Historicist school of thought taught that the Beast of Revelation was a symbol of the Roman Papacy. It was this interpretation that was later adopted by the Reformation fathers of the 14th to 16th centuries. This list includes such worthies as:

John Wycliff 1329-1384 - The "Morning Star of the Reformation"
John Knox 1514-1572 - Scottish Presbyterian Reformer
William Tyndale 1494-1536- Reformer, Bible translator, martyr
Martin Luther 1483-1546 - German Reformer
John Calvin 1509-1536 - French theologian and Reformer
Ulrich Zwingli 1484-1531 - Swiss Reformer
Philip Melanchthon 1497-1560 - wrote the Augsburg Confession
Sir Isaac Newton 1642-1727 - English Scientist and Bible Scholar
John Huss 1373-1415 - Bohemian Reformer

John Foxe 1516-1587 - wrote "Foxe's Book of Martyrs"
John Wesley 1703-1791 - Father of Methodism
Jonathan Edwards 1703-1758 - Pastor,"First Great Awakening"
George Whitefield 1714-1770 - English Evangelist
Charles G. Finney 1792-1875 - American Evangelist
Charles H. Spurgeon 1834-1892 - English Baptist Pastor
Matthew Henry 1662-1714 - Welsh Bible Scholar

The above names are far from being a complete list of great Bible scholars, pastors and evangelists who believed the Historicist approach to prophecy with some lasting through the 19th century and well into the 20th century. The advocates of Historicism view the seventy weeks of Daniel as being completely fulfilled in the old Judah nation and ending in 34 AD. It also views the Book of Revelation as portraying a survey of the overall history of the Christian Church. It would include the major events of European history including the Roman Empire, Papal Rome, the rise of Mohammedanism, the Protestant Reformation, the development of Christian Western Civilization and the future consummation of God's plan of the ages in the city of New Jerusalem of Revelation 21-22.

For a more thorough explanation of the Historicist interpretation and the book of Revelation please order the book entitled, *"The Book of Revelation - From an Israelite and Historicist Interpretation"* which is available from this ministry.

With the brutality and iniquity of the Papacy being exposed for so long through the powerful influence of the Reformers, Rome was forced to do something to counter-act this campaign in order to maintain its strangle-hold on the common people and monarchs of Europe. A short and clear explanation is given in the book, **Revelation - Four Views, a Parallel Commentary**, edited by Steve Gregg. Pp 31-32.

"Coming to the defense of the papacy, Spanish Jesuits presented two alternative approaches to the historicism of the Reformers. One response was that of Francisco Ribera (1537-1591), a professor at Salamanca,(Spain) who taught that John in Revelation only foresaw events of the near future and of the final things at the end of the world, but had none of the intervening history in view. The antichrist was defined as a future individual who would arise in the end times. Babylon was seen as Rome - not under the popes - but in a future corrupted state. This was the beginning of many of the ideas that are now a part of the Futurist approach to Revelation."

In 1826, the Librarian to the Archbishop of Canterbury, S.R. Maitland discovered Francisco Ribera's writings and published them. This theory of the postponement of the antichirst and the tribulation period into the future had already been taught for 250 years by the Jesuits. To add fuel to the fire of ***Futurism,*** another Jesuit named Emanuel Lacunza published his book entitled, *"The Coming of the Messiah in Glory and Majesty"* in 1816. Lacunza, along with other fellow Jesuits, had been expelled from Chile for their encouragement of treachery and violence. He wrote his book under the name of "Rabbi Ben Ezra," a supposedly converted Jew. He added a prayer asking the Almighty to use his book for the enlightenment of the Jewish people. Lacunza set forth the theory that Jesus was to have a future two stage coming; once *for* His saints and then *with* His saints at a later date. The ultimate result of the writings of Ribera and Lacunza were that **1)** the events of Revelation 4:1 and following were to take place in the future; **2)** the appearance of the Antichrist and the two witnesses and relative prophecies also in the future; **3)** all these prophetic events are scheduled to transpire in a very short space of seven years between the first and second comings of Jesus; **4)** the rapture of the church is to take place as a future event which will be the starting point for all the other events to follow.

Lacunza's book came into the hands of Edward Irving, a young and brilliant Scottish Presbyterian minister during the 1820's. He accepted the task of translation of this devious theory from Spanish into English. Irving was aware of the true identity of Lacunza as being a Spanish Jesuit and not a converted Jewish Rabbi. Still, he continued to translate and publish a theory that would turn out to be one of the most detrimental misconceptions of Scripture in the 2,000 year history of the Christian Church. When he published his English version in London in 1827, he claimed he heard a voice telling him to preach a secret rapture of the church with the two-stage theory of Christ's future comings.

In 1830, Margaret MacDonald, a young Scottish lassie supposedly had a revelation by means of a 'vision' from God. In her 'vision' she saw Jesus coming in a secret rapture to remove the righteous saints from planet earth. At the time she was attending a church that was connected with the Brethren Movement of which Edward Irving was closely associated. Naturally, Irving seized upon this 'vision' as a witness to his teaching and began to spread this theory even more enthusiastically.

In 1833 in the city of London, meetings were being conducted by some Irvingite followers. Among those invited to the meetings was John Nelson Darby, who possessed a keen interest in prophecy and had exceptional writing skills. Soon he became convinced of the Irvingite teaching of a secret rapture and other Futuristic interpretations of prophecy originated long before by the Jesuits. Darby began to publish and distribute his new found secret rapture theory. He eventually made five trips to the United States and convinced many new converts, among them being Cyrus Ingerson (C.I.) Scofield, a one-time law student turned 'preacher.' This new theory of prophetic interpretation was introduced to the Bible conferences that were being conducted in the late 19th century. From this venue was the springboard for advancing this theory to the American evangelical church world.

> "I will venture to assert that - there is not a Bible teacher nor anyone else living in the world today who has found a secret rapture in the Bible by his own independent study of the Bible itself. These teachers all come to the Bible with cut-and-dried theories which they have learnt elsewhere, and twist and torture texts to fit the theory. If the spiritual pedigree of the Futurist Bible teachers could be traced back, they would all be found to spring from one source - Lacunza - the Jesuit."
>
> Duncan McDougall
"The Rapture of the Saints"
>
> (Duncan McDougall was one of Scotland's well-known Gaelic scholars holding linguistic degrees in Latin, Greek, Hebrew and Gaelic.)

Historical records show that the personal, family and business life of C. I. Scofield included dishonest business practices, unpaid debts and refusal to support his wife and family. This was only a part of the immoral character of the man who was to later publish a study Bible that would influence multiplied millions of Christians world-wide. For a complete history of his life and work read Joseph M. Canfield's book entitled, ***"The Incredible Scofield."*** (This book is not available from this ministry.) With the sponsorship of James H. Brookes, a die-hard Darbyite, and later the leadership of Arno C. Gaebelein, Scofield was accepted into the fellowship of the Bible conferences at Niagara Falls, New York. It was here and other conferences where the "lost truth" of Futurism was hammered out. Scofield developed his notes to place in the margins of his now famous Bible. The Scofield marginal notes to millions of unsuspecting Christians have become as sacred as the Word of God itself. Thus the historical trail of the prophetic interpretation of a vast number of "Protestants" today can be easily traced to the Jesuit priests, Emanuel Lacunza, Francisco Ribera and company.

> "The rapture doctrine is a false teaching that Jesus warned us to expect in the latter days."
>
> Corrie Ten Boom
>
> From *"Rapture - Prophecy or Heresy"* by H. Speed Wilson p. 74

False Hope

Throughout the development of the Futurist interpretation of prophecy, the advocates of this false theory have capitalized on certain 'future' events which they feel are extremely critical. They include the Mark of the Beast, a one-world government and church, (which they are ignorantly helping to create), the establishment of the Zionist State of Israel as being the fulfillment of Bible prophecy, the present day Jewish people as being the totality of all twelve tribes of Israel, a seven year tribulation period, and their highly prized lucrative doctrine, the secret rapture of the church. In their fervor to promote this theory (which many truly born-again saints sincerely believe, yet never researched) they have used many Bible passages as part of their support system. The following are just a few:

Revelation 4:1

"After this I looked, and, behold, a door was opened in heaven: and the first voice which I heard was as it were of a trumpet talking with me; which said, Come up hither, and I will shew thee things which must be hereafter."

The experience that John the Revelator records here has been mistakenly used to teach the timing of the rapture as being just before the beginning of "the tribulation." This call to John to *"come up hither"* is supposedly the call for all the saints to rise up to their eternal home. When honestly reading this text, there is no indication whatsoever that there is any rapture at all taking place. This call to John applied only to him to rise in spiritual ecstasy in order to receive revelations about coming events.

Paul the Apostle records in II Corinthians 12:2-4 that he *"knew a man in Christ above fourteen years ago, (whether in the body I cannot tell; or whether out of the body, I cannot tell: God knoweth:) such an one caught up to the third heaven. . . How that he was caught up into paradise..."* This was a very similar experience like John, yet the rapture teachers never use this passage to prove their theory. If John's experience was a type of the rapture, why isn't Paul's experience a type of the same alleged rapture? These were supernatural experiences to individuals for the purpose of receiving divine revelations.

Matthew 24:36-42

"But of that day and hour knoweth no man, no, not the angels of heaven, but my Father only. But as the days of Noe were, so shall also the coming of the Son of man be. For as in the days that were before the flood they were eating and drinking, marrying and giving in marriage, until the day that Noe entered into the ark, And knew not until the flood came, and took them all away; so shall also

the coming of the Son of man be. Then shall two be in the field; the one shall be taken, and the other left. Two women shall be grinding at the mill; the one shall be taken, and the other left. Watch therefore: for ye know not what hour your Lord doth come."

The phrase, *"the one shall be taken and the other left"* has been widely used to mean that the saints are "taken" in the rapture and the wicked are left behind to endure the horrors of the tribulation. When any elementary Bible student reads the text concerning the days of Noah in verses 37-39, it is evident which ones are taken. It is not the righteous ones, Noah and his family, that were taken away in the flood. **For sure, Jesus Christ is coming again.** When He returns it is not the righteous that He is going to remove, but the wicked. Our Lord's lesson of the removal of the wicked **first** is very evident in the parable of the wheat and the tares in Matthew 13:24-30, 36-43. Jesus said that during the harvest at the end of the age the angels shall **first** gather the tares out of His kingdom and burn them. Then the righteous shall shine forth in the Kingdom of their Father. Paul the Apostle wrote to the Thessalonian saints and set the record straight.

II Thessalonians 1:7-10
"And to you who are troubled rest with us, when the Lord Jesus shall be revealed from heaven with his mighty angels, In flaming fire taking vengeance on them that know not God, and that obey not the gospel of our Lord Jesus Christ: Who shall be punished with everlasting destruction from the presence of the Lord, and from the glory of his power; When he shall come to be glorified in his saints, and to be admired in all them that believe (because our testimony among you was believed) in that day."

I Thessalonians 5:9
"For God hath not appointed us to wrath, but to obtain salvation by our Lord Jesus Christ."

I once asked a professor of Dispensational Futurism for proof of the pre-trib rapture theory. The professor was a genuine born-again believer, highly educated with more than one doctorate degree and very qualified in his field of study. He was setting forth the party-line of pre-tribulation rapture. My question was; "Doctor, what concrete biblical evidence is there for believing that the Christians will be raptured away before the tribulation to avoid the wrath of God that is poured out during that time?" With a puzzled look on his face, and contemplating a minute concerning his answer, he said, "The only real evidence I can think of is, 'God hath not appointed us to wrath.'"

Ever since that day I have wondered how does that apply to the thousands of first-century saints who became martyrs to whom that admonition was written. How does that fit with the sixty million Christians martyred under the heavy hand of Papal Rome, the multiplied thousands of saints who were murdered under the dictates of Josef Stalin or the untold number of believers who died without mercy during the communist takeover of China in 1948? Several years ago an interview with Corrie Ten Boom was recorded where she stated that during World War II when Northern Europe was being overrun by invading military forces and Christians brutalized, many Christians ran to their pastors and asked them, "Where is the Rapture?" The pastors had no answer and the saints had been living with a false hope.

When these facts are pointed out to a rapturist teacher, their immediate rebuttal is; "Well, that means Christians sometimes suffer the wrath of man, but not the wrath of God and the tribulation is God's wrath and not man's." Yet these same rapture teachers tell us that during the tribulation the Antichrist will have complete control and kill those who "have the testimony of Jesus Christ." What about the souls under the altar crying for vengeance in Revelation 6:9-11?

What about the saints "which came out of great tribulation" in Revelation 7:9-17? Surely, they endured the wrath of man during the time when the pre-tribulation rapturist declare that this will be a time of the wrath of God. Under close scrutiny of logic and the searchlight of the Scriptures, the pre-trib rapture theory and all its props simply are washed away like a sand castle during high tide.

I Thessalonians 4:13-17

"But I would not have you to be ignorant, brethren, concerning them which are asleep, that ye sorrow not, even as others which have no hope. For if we believe that Jesus died and rose again, even so them also which sleep in Jesus will God bring with him. For this we say unto you by the word of the Lord, that we which are alive and remain unto the coming of the Lord shall not prevent them which are asleep. For the Lord himself shall descend from heaven with a shout, with the voice of the archangel, and with the trump of God: and the dead in Christ shall rise first: Then we which are alive and remain shall be caught up together with them in the clouds, to meet the Lord in the air: and so shall we ever be with the Lord."

From this and other Scriptural passages it is evident the Bible teaches that ***Jesus Christ is coming again***. When He descends, He comes to remain on the earth and remove out of His kingdom that which offends and works iniquity (Matt. 13:41). The angel Gabriel told Mary that her son Jesus, shall be given the throne of His father David and He shall reign over the House of Jacob forever (Luke 1:31-33). This definitely sounds like He will be reigning here on the earth forever. Even Jesus taught His disciples to pray, *"Thy kingdom come, Thy will be done in earth as it is in heaven"*(Matt. 6:9-10). Paul the Apostle wrote words of comforting expectation to Titus when he said *"Looking for that blessed hope, and the glorious appearing of the great God and our Saviour Jesus Christ"* (Titus 2:13).

When Paul wrote to the saints at Thessalonica, he was addressing one of their major concerns. That was, the state of the righteous dead. He then assures the living saints that their Christian loved ones will not be forgotten by the Lord when He comes again. Their bodies will be resurrected as he stated in I Cor. 15:15-57. The Apostle declares that when Jesus returns He will bring the spirits of all the sleeping saints with Him. In I Thess. 4:15-17, he reassures the hope of the living saints by saying that:

1) The resurrection of the living saints will not prevent (the old English word for 'precede') or take place before the resurrection of the sleeping saints.

2) The Lord Himself shall descend from heaven with a very loud arrival announcement – a shout, the voice of the archangel and the trump of God. There will be nothing secret or quiet about His arrival (see II Thess. 1:7-8, Matt. 24:31). Where is the 'secret rapture' mentioned in this verse where family members will quietly disappear without notice?

3) Then the bodies of the living saints at Jesus' coming shall be changed (I Cor.15:51-54) into an incorruptible body and they shall possess a glorified body like unto their Lord.

4) This latter group of living saints shall then be 'caught up' or removed from their present state of being to join the former group of 'sleeping' saints. The Lord Jesus is **_not_** returning alone. Jude says that *"Behold the Lord cometh with ten thousands of His saints"* (Jude 14). This vast company of saints is what comprises the *'clouds'* of I Thess. 4:17. The 'living' saints shall join this vast *'cloud of witnesses'* (Heb. 12:1) while meeting the Lord *'in the air.'* The writer of Hebrews clearly applies the 'cloud' of witnesses to the **people** that he listed in chapter eleven. *"In the air"* denotes the location of the state of elevated and spiritual union with the 'sleeping' saints and with the Lord Jesus. This Scriptural passage which is used as the main stronghold of the rapturists says absolutely nothing about flying away to another planet called heaven. If there is a 'rapture' to any degree at all, the saints will only go up as far as the air extends. 'Air' is the elastic and invisible mixture of several gases (nitrogen, oxygen, hydrogen, etc) that surrounds the earth. This is the atmosphere of space above the earth's surface. How far up from the earth's surface does the air extend? Then that would be the extent of their distance of travel. It would be less than seven miles.

The writer Jude also gives us the **_purpose_** for which the Lord returns. He says, *"To execute judgment upon all, and to convince all that are ungodly among them of all their ungodly deeds which they have ungodly committed, and of all their hard speeches which ungodly sinners have spoken against him"* (Jude 15).

The Bible teaches that there will be just *one* future glorious, visible, physical and audible coming of our Lord; **1)** to execute judgment upon the ungodly, and **2)** to be glorified in His saints (II Thess. 1:7-10).

False Predictions

Among all the hype that is generated as a result of the prophetic theory of Futurism are false predictions and vain speculations. The false predictions concerning the time of the rapture is nothing new. Men who claimed they had special knowledge and insight into the future have mustered a devoted group of followers around themselves have felt 'safe' in making outlandish predictions. The predictions of the timing of the coming of Jesus to 'snatch away His bride' have ranged from 1844 to present. The basis for many of the false predictions have been things such as; the measurements between various points inside the Great Pyramid of Giza in Egypt, the religious, social, economic and political "signs of the times," the word 'generation' used by our Lord in Matthew 24:34, the date of May 14, 1948, which was the establishment of the modern Zionist state of Israel, etc.

In 1987 there was one brave rapture teacher that was bold enough to publicly proclaim the date of the rapture as May 14, 1988. He based his predictions upon the 40th anniversary of the modern Zionist State which he so rashly proclaimed as the fulfillment of Bible prophecy. There was a later prediction of September 1988. Needless to say, both predictions failed. To my knowledge, the latest date that has been predicted by one of the most publicly acclaimed prophecy 'experts' is 2007 to 2012. At least he is smart enough to give a five year window of escape.

Vain speculations have also been a tragic result in the wake of Futurism's captivating influence. For many years Futurist teachers have attempted to identify who the Antichrist would be. At one time Mussolini was the likely candidate, but after the people strung him up by his heels, then Hitler was their choice. Some even thought it was Franklin D. Roosevelt. Some 'experts' are for certain that the Antichrist must be a Jew, while others assure their supporters that he will be of Oriental descent. Others are certain that the Antichirst will be a man of Western Europe in order to rule over the ten nations of the Revived Roman Empire. All these false predictions and vain speculations are a direct result of twisting, distorting and even raping the sacred Scriptures. Our modern day 'protestant' evangelical church world has fallen in step with the schemes of the Jesuit's counter-reformation.

The Antichrist

Who is the Antichrist? Where will he come from? When will he be revealed? What supernatural powers will he display? Has he already been born? These and a host of other questions are now the topic of books, sermons, seminars and conferences being sponsored by last day prophecy gurus. They have thoroughly convinced the vast majority of modern day Christendom to the extent that they are infatuated with this unknown charismatic character. According to the Futurists, this mysterious one-man epitome of evil has been designated in Scripture by many descriptive names such as; the little horn, the man of sin, the idol shepherd, the Assyrian, the prince that shall come, and 'he' of Daniel 9:27, etc.

The real question is; "Does the Bible really teach a future one-man Antichrist?" The term *'antichrist'* is only found in the Bible five times. In none of these five places does it refer to a one-man antichrist. In considering these five references where this term is used, an honest minded Bible student must consider the times and conditions in which they occurred. The Apostle John is writing his first general epistle and makes reference to the many people in his day that once identified themselves with the early church, but were not genuine Christian believers. They were antichrist.

I John 2:18-19

"Little children, it is the last time: and as ye have heard that antichrist shall come, even now are there many antichrists; whereby we know that it is the last time. They went out from us, but they were not of us; for if they had been of us, they would no doubt have continued with us: but they went out, that they might be made manifest that they were not all of us."

The two references to 'antichrist' in verse 18 refer to people in John's day that were once numbered with John and the other believers. For some reason they had left the fellowship of believers. John points out, that because they left the fellowship, that was proof they were never genuine believers to start with. They were possibly Judaizers in the church for the purpose of perverting the saints from their belief in the sovereign grace of God and the total sufficiency of the cross-work of Jesus Christ.

I John 2:22-23

"Who is a liar but he that denieth that Jesus is the Christ? He is antichrist, that denieth the Father and the Son. Whosoever denieth the Son, the same hath not the Father: [but] he that acknowledgeth the Son hath the Father also."

Here in this reference, John identifies anyone who denies the divinity of Jesus Christ as being antichrist. He also calls them a liar. There were many false teachers in John's day who traveled from church to church teaching perverse things about the person and work of Jesus Christ. Many denied that Jesus was the true Messiah and therefore John considered them antichrist.

I John 4:1-3

"Beloved, believe not every spirit, but try the spirits whether they are of God: because many false prophets are gone out into the world. Hereby know ye the Spirit of God: Every spirit that confesseth that Jesus Christ is come in the flesh is of God: And every spirit that confesseth not that Jesus Christ is come in the flesh is not of God: and this is that spirit of antichrist, whereof ye have heard that it should come; and even now already is it in the world."

Here John gives a warning to beware of these same false teachers. John was the same writer who told us that *"The Word became flesh and dwelt among us..."* John 1:14. John labeled this teaching as being the *'spirit of antichrist.'* He emphasized that this was a **'spirit'** and not just an individual person. He said *"believe not every spirit,"* *"try the spirits"* (v. 1), *"every spirit that confesseth not"* (v. 3). He said that *"spirit"* was already in the world in his day and that has been well over 1900 years ago.

II John 7

"For many deceivers are entered into the world, who confess not that Jesus Christ is come in the flesh. This is a deceiver and an antichrist."

Here again John is warning the believers to beware of the many deceivers that existed in his day. These false teachers were considered deceivers and antichrist. Never once in the above five references to *antichrist* did John refer to: **1)** "The" Antichrist; **2)** one individual man; **3)** or a future appearance.

John did refer to antichrist as being: **1)** a spirit (I John 4:3); **2)** a denial of the incarnation of God in Christ (I John 4:2); **3)** already present in his day (I John 2:18; 4:3) **4)** Liars who denied that Jesus is the Christ (I John 2:22); **5)** deceivers (II John 7); **6)** there were many who were antichrist (I John 2:18); **7)** false believers who left the fellowship (I John 2:19).

Seventy Weeks of Daniel

One of the many serious errors of Futurism is built upon a misconstruing of the message of the angel Gabriel to the prophet Daniel. Futurism teachers have naively fallen in line with the Jesuit theory that the seventieth week of Daniel's prophecy has been separated from the first sixty nine weeks. This position is taken in order to create a time-line for their whole prophetic scheme. This time period between the sixty-ninth and seventieth weeks is conveniently called, the gap or parenthesis. This period is characterized by the 'age of grace' during the church age! This period of approximately 2000 years is when God is dealing with the people they call 'Gentiles,' which according to the Futurist teachers is everyone that is not a Jew. They promote the idea that during this so-called 'Church age' the Lord is mainly calling the Gentile people to form His 'Gentile Bride' while allowing the vast majority of the Jewish people to remain untouched by the Gospel. They say that immediately after the 'Gentile Bride' is raptured away, then Jewish evangelism will explode with astounding success.

Where do the advocates of such man-made ideas get their audacity to arbitrarily cut-off one 'week' from a calendar and build a complete prophetic viewpoint on that one false presupposition? Upon this one false premise they do more injustice to Scripture by claiming that 'he' of Daniel 9:27 refers to a future antichrist. It is clear from the whole context of Daniel's prophecy that the 'he' refers back to the Messiah in verse 26, which was to be cut off. This is plainly referring to the crucifixion of our Lord at Calvary. Gabriel's message to Daniel goes on to say that 'he' (the

Messiah), shall *"confirm the covenant with many for one week."* The confirming of a covenant is what Jeremiah referred to in his prophecy. He proclaimed, *"Behold, the days come, saith the LORD, that I will make a new covenant with the house of Israel, and with the house of Judah: Not according to the covenant that I made with their fathers in the day that I took them by the hand to bring them out of the land of Egypt; which my covenant they brake, although I was an husband unto them, saith the LORD: But this shall be the covenant that I will make with the house of Israel; After those days, saith the LORD, I will put my law in their inward parts, and write it in their hearts; and will be their God, and they shall be my people. And they shall teach no more every man his neighbour, and every man his brother, saying, Know the LORD: for they shall all know me, from the least of them unto the greatest of them, saith the LORD: for I will forgive their iniquity, and I will remember their sin no more."*

Jeremiah 31:31-34

The writer of the Book of Hebrews repeats Jeremiah's prophecy and clearly applied it to the making and confirmation of the **New Covenant** (Heb. 8:6-13). This is the New Covenant that Jesus ratified with the sacrifice of His own blood. As our Melchisedec priest, during the last Passover meal with His disciples, our Savior affirmed the fact that by the shedding of His blood a new covenant was made. He said, *"For this is my blood of the New Testament (covenant), which is shed for many for the remission of sins"* (Matthew 26:26-28).

The angelic messenger plainly stated the six-fold purpose of this seventy weeks or 490 year period. The Messianic purpose was:

1) to finish the transgression - Isaiah 53:5, Hebrews 10:12-14
2) to make an end of sins - Hebrews 9:26
3) to make reconciliation for iniquity - Rom. 5:10, Heb. 10:17

4) to bring in everlasting righteousness - II Corinthians 5:21
5) to seal up the vision and prophecy - Matthew 5:17
6) to anoint the Most Holy - Luke 4:18; Acts 10:38

The anointing of the Most Holy refers to Jesus Christ when He was anointed at His water baptism which marked the beginning of the seventieth week of Daniel. In Mark 1:15 Jesus said, *"The time is fulfilled. . ."* referring to the beginning of His public ministry and His work of redemption on the cross for His people. In the middle of the seventieth week the Messiah (Jesus Christ) was 'cut off' or crucified (Daniel 9:26-27). At His crucifixion Jesus caused the Levitical sacrifices to cease and made reconciliation for our sins (Daniel 9:24, 27). Through Biblical exegesis and a basic understanding of history, it is very evident that *all* seventy weeks were completely fulfilled. Nowhere in this prophecy does it make reference to:

1) a one-man Antichrist;
2) a rebuilt temple in Jerusalem;
3) "the" Antichrist making a covenant with the Jews;
4) "the" Antichrist breaking a covenant;
5) the 70th week of Daniel being separated from the 69th week with a 'gap' of 2000 years.

The Two Witnesses

In Revelation 11:3-12 is described the two witnesses with their work, their death and their resurrection. From the fundamentalist, Futuristic interpretation of Bible prophecy, it is commonly taught that the two witnesses are two men of the Old Testament era that have been resurrected or either the two men that did not die and therefore are brought back into their physical bodies and placed on this earth. Ordinarily, it is believed that the two witnesses are either Moses and Elijah, Elijah and Enoch or Moses and Enoch. There is quite a dispute over the difference of opinion as to which of the two men of these three it will be.

First, let us ascertain from the Old Testament who God refers to as His two witnesses. In Isaiah 43:10 it is stated unto Jacob which is inclusive of both houses of Israel, *"Ye are my witnesses saith God and my servant whom I have chosen. . ."* The prophet is referring to Jacob, yet he says, ye are my witnesses, which denotes a plurality of witnesses. In Isaiah 44:8 it is stated, *"Fear ye not, neither be afraid: have not I told thee from that time, and have declared it? Ye are even my witnesses."* God is speaking to Jacob His servant, that the family of Jacob are His witnesses. In Revelation 11:3 the possessive personal pronoun "my" is used again as it was in both Scriptures in Isaiah. Does the Lord have different witnesses than what is stated in the Old Testament? No, His witnesses would be the same. In Psalm 114:2 the Psalmist speaks of Judah as being the Lord's **sanctuary** while Israel as being His **dominion.** This denotes a two-fold office of religious and civil authority within the family of Jacob.

In Revelation 11:4 we are given a strong clue as to the identity of these two witnesses by the reference to the two olive trees and the two candlesticks standing before the God of the whole earth. In Haggai 1:1 and 14 is mentioned two men and their respective offices which were instrumental in the restoration of the city of Jerusalem after the Babylonian exile. Joshua the High Priest and Zerubbabel the Governor are the two men which are types of the two witnesses of Revelation 11. It is very significant to remember that the two God-given institutions that were reestablished during this post-exilic era were **civil authority** under Zerubbabel the Governor and **religious authority** under Joshua the High Priest. The parallel remains the same. Those two institutions are civil authority and religious authority under the dual office of the Messiah originally intended to be exercised through His Church in His Kingdom. Someday Jesus Christ will execute full authority in both of these offices as is reflected in His title, King of kings and Lord of lords.

While allowing the Scriptures to speak for themselves, we are given a clear understanding who the two witnesses are. While following the Futuristic scheme, 'Protestants' remain in darkness and once again bow to the bidding of the Jesuits.

The Tragic Aftermath of Futurism

When one considers the origin of Futurism and its tragic results, the words of our Lord so clearly apply: *"an enemy hath done this"* (Matt. 13:28). The tragic aftermath has been a major departure from our historic Protestant faith. The false predictions and vain speculations about the future have diverted Christians from the centrality of Christ to a daily political watch. The high profile rapturists have become nothing more than newspaper 'prophets' for profit. Prophecy has become a lucrative economic market. Hard core Dispensational Futurism in its blind devotion to the modern political Zionist State of Israel is redefining Christianity into a religious, political and military campaign to bring about their desired Armageddon. By this they intend to speed up the rapture for the saints, which is utterly ridiculous.

The timing for the coming of Christ is reserved and determined by God alone (Acts 1:7). Modern apostate Christianity, along with Zionistic Judaism and radical Islam are the *"three unclean spirits like frogs"* (Rev. 16:13-14) gathering the nations to battle.

Very influential Dispensational Futurist ministers are helping to determine our national foreign policy, especially in Middle Eastern affairs. In their misguided zeal, they are calling for a war of "end-time apocalyptic" proportions with Islam in order to protect the modern political Zionist State. They view political Zionism as fulfillment of Bible prophecy while being totally captivated by the Jewish "God's chosen people" myth.

Futurism also advocates a rebuilt Jewish temple including the Levitical animal sacrifices. In order to expedite the building of this new temple and the reinstitution of animal sacrifices, " run-away" Futurists are on the look-out for a perfect red heifer. Some American cattle ranchers are feverishly working through scientific means to produce a red heifer. Nowhere does the Bible teach there will be a rebuilt Jewish temple. The Body of Christ, the Church is the true temple (*naos*) of God: *"Know ye not that ye are the temple of God?"* (I Corinthians 3:16-17; 6:19-20). The whole context of the Book of Hebrews tells us that there is only one sacrifice for sin. That is the substitutionary death and blood sacrifice of Jesus Christ (Hebrews 7:27; 9:6-15, 28). Any other blood sacrifice for any reason would be blasphemy and insult to the Spirit of Grace and the blood of Jesus. The advocates of this practice are those *". . .who hath trodden under foot the Son of God, and hath counted the blood of the covenant, wherewith he was sanctified, an unholy thing, and hath done despite* [insult] *unto the Spirit of grace?"* (Hebrews 10:26-29).

The Futurist approach to the prophecy of Scripture does an enormous injustice, not only to proper Biblical exegesis, but also common sense in understanding the development of human affairs. Its unrealistic attempt to squeeze the vast majority of Revelation events into seven short years with a strict literal application defies both logic and Biblical typology. Though it is this interpretation that is the most popular and financially rewarding. When one understands the Historical viewpoint of the Book of Revelation, as the prophetic outline of the history of God's true covenant people Israel, it brings all of prophecy into proper focus.

Nowhere does the Bible teach a rapture of the saints to fly away to another planet called heaven. What the Bible does teach is that Jesus Christ is returning to this earth to remain. He will then possess His Kingdom. The resurrection of the saints will take place as He returns in glory and power. *His coming results in resurrection and immortality, not in a rapture.*

The whole teaching of Jesuit inspired Futurism has tragically resulted in: **1)** the forsaking of true Biblical prophecy and chronology, **2)** blinding the church as to who God's true people Israel are, **3)** a departure from the Protestant faith of our forefathers, **4)** accepting an alternative means of salvation for the Jewish people, **5)** a theology of abdication of God's sovereign power to "the Antichrist," **6)** an attitude of apathy and defeat while waiting for "escape," **7)** total ignorance of Christ's coming kingdom reign of righteousness on the earth (Luke 1:30-33).

The main purpose of prophetic utterances of Scripture is not to generate fear and uncertainty about the future, but to reveal the Lord Jesus Christ in all His glory and majesty. All true prophecy glorifies our Lord Jesus, because *"the testimony of Jesus is the* [true] *spirit of prophecy"* (Rev. 19:10).

Truth in History Ministries is the evangelistic outreach of *The Bible Educator Ministry* and is a Christ centered and Bible based ministry proclaiming the Lordship of Jesus Christ and His sovereign control of human history as taught in the Holy Scriptures. It is our mission and purpose to proclaim Jesus Christ as our only Savior, Healer, Baptizer, Sanctifier and coming King; to teach the Holy Scriptures in order to edify Christian believers and strengthen local churches. We endeavor to proclaim this message through the means of a web site, printed literature, sermon tapes and other available electronic media for the glory and honor of Jesus Christ. We believe and proclaim Jesus Christ as our **Prophet, Priest and King!**

Pastor Charles A. Jennings

The Bible Educator Ministry
Web site: www.thebibleeducator.org

"Where the Word of God is not Bound"

For a free catalog of other available material and television broadcasting schedule please contact:

Truth in History Ministries
P.O. Box 808
Owasso, Oklahoma 74055-0808
web site: www.truthinhistory.org
E-mail: charles@truthinhistory.org